THE LITTLE
JOKE BOOK

ILLUSTRATED BY HENRY R. MARTIN

THE PETER PAUPER PRESS
Mount Vernon, New York

COPYRIGHT
©
1959
BY THE
PETER
PAUPER
PRESS

The Little
Joke Book

"Doctor, what should a man take when he is run down?"

"The license number, sir, the license number."

"Name four animals of the cat family."
"The father cat, the mother cat, and two kittens."

"My wife has the worst memory I ever heard of."

"Forgets everything, eh?"

"No; remembers everything."

"My sister is awfully lucky," said little Bobby to his friend.

"Why?"

"She went to a party last night and they played a game where the boys had to kiss the girl or else pay her a box of chocolates."

"Well, how was your sister lucky?"

"She came home with ten boxes of chocolates."

Wife — "Is it true that money talks?"
Husband — "That's what they say."
Wife — "Well, leave a little here to talk to me today. I get so lonely."

"Children, give me a proverb about parents. First, one about a father."

One little girl put up her hand. "There's no fool like an old fool," she said.

The teacher had been talking about the weather peculiarities of March. "What is it," she asked, "that comes in like a lion and goes out like a lamb?"

A little girl in the back row replied: "Father."

"What is puppy love?"
"It's the beginning of a dog's life."

Director — "That Indian wants two hundred dollars to act the part."
Producer — "Give him a hundred. We need only a half-breed."

A backwoodsman was watching a store clerk open a package of gaily colored men's pajamas.

"What's them?" he asked.
"Pajamas."
"Pajamas?" echoed the woodsman. "What are they for?"
"Why, you wear them nights," the clerk explained. "Want to buy a pair?"
"Not me," said the woodsman. "I don't go nowhere nights except to bed."

The sun never sets on the British Empire because the British Empire is in the East and the sun sets in the West.

"My husband is crazy about me. He says such nice things in his sleep. But it's a funny thing — he always calls me by the wrong name."

An Indian reservation is a place that consists of a mile of land for every five square Indians.

A sincere friend is one who says nasty things to your face, instead of saying them behind your back.

Nero was a cruel Emperor who would torture his poor subjects by playing the fiddle to them.

"I sure hope I'm sick," said the miserable man to his doctor. "I'd hate to feel this way if I'm well."

A mountain pass is a pass given by railroads to its employees so that they can spend their vacation in the mountains.

"Mother," said the boy, "will you help me with some words? Is it correct to say you 'water a horse' when he's thirsty?"

"Yes, quite correct."

"Then," said the boy picking up a saucer, "I'm going to milk the cat."

"My husband certainly does enjoy smoking in his den. Does your husband have a den?"

"No, he growls all over the house."

"They always said that old man Jones was good to his folks."

"Yes, he was indeed! He was hardly ever home."

A conceited actor was boasting: "Why, at every performance, during the last act, I have the audience glued to their seats!"

"Oh, my!" exclaimed his friend. "How clever of you to think of it!"

Jane — "Mother, are you the nearest relative I've got?"

Mother — "Yes, dear, and your father is the closest."

Hubby — "You call that a hat? My dear, I'll never stop laughing."

Wifey — "Oh, yes you will and I'll tell you when: the bill will arrive tomorrow."

Lady — "My good man, does your firm allow you to take tips?"
Delivery Boy — "No, lady, but if they asked if you gave me one, I'd lie like anything to save you."

"Jones, how late do you usually sleep on Sunday morning?"
"It all depends."
"Depends on what?"
"The length of the sermon."

"But," protested the new arrival, as St. Peter handed him a golden trumpet, "I can't play this instrument; I never played any instrument on earth."
"Of course you didn't," chuckled the saint. "That's why you are here."

Lady — "And has your baby learned to talk yet?"
New Father — "Oh my, yes. We're teaching him to keep quiet now."

Your Conscience is the still small voice that makes you feel still smaller.

"Why don't you settle the case out of court?" said the judge to the litigants before him.

"Sure, that's just what we were doing, Your Honor, when the police came."

Transparent means something you can see through, like a keyhole.

An insurance agent was teaching his wife to drive, when the brakes suddenly failed going down a hill.

"I can't stop it," she cried. "What'll I do?"

"Don't panic," said her husband, "just hit something cheap."

Advertising man — "Would you endorse our cigarette for two thousand dollars?"

Movie Actor — "Man, for two thousand dollars I'd even smoke them!"

Degrees of comparison of "Bad."
Bad: very sick: dead.
Bad: badder: burst.

Mother — "Who ever taught you to use that dreadful, dreadful word you just said, Danny dear?"
Danny — "Santa Claus, mama."
Mother — "Santa Claus?"
Danny — "Yes, mama, when he fell over a chair in my room the night before Christmas."

"Say, that's a bad wound on your forehead. How did you get it?"

"I bit myself."

"Come, come; how could you bite yourself on the forehead?"

"I stood on a chair."

An elegantly-dressed gentleman got out of his Cadillac and sat down at the counter of a little diner out West.

"Do you like split-pea soup?" asked the waiter.

"No," said the man.

"Chicken croquettes?"

"No."

"Prune pie?"

"No."

The waiter flicked his cloth. "Goodbye," he said. "You've had your lunch."

Teacher — "Now we are going to study the water birds. Of course, the stork is the biggest — what are you laughing at, Gertrude?"

Gertrude — "Oh *teacher* — the idea of there *being* any storks!"

"Darling," said the bride as the honeymooners drove up to their hotel, "let's try to act like we've been married for years."

"Okay, sweetie," said the groom, "but do you think you can carry the suitcases?"

Judge — "Have you anything to offer the court in your favor before sentence is passed?"

Prisoner — "No, Your Honor, my lawyer took my last dollar."

A beautiful blonde walked into a Chicago police station and gave the desk sergeant a detailed description of a man who had dragged her by the hair down three flights of stairs, threatened to choke her to death and finally beat her up.

"With that description, we'll have him arrested and put in jail in practically no time," said the desk sergeant.

"But I don't want him arrested," the young woman protested. "Just find him for me. He promised to marry me."

A man was trying to teach his wife to drive. She was very nervous. All at once she screamed:

"What do I do? Here comes a telephone pole!"

Judge—"You stole eggs from this man's store. Have you any explanation?"
Accused — "Yes, Your Honor, I took them by mistake."
Judge — "How is that?"
Accused—"I thought they were fresh."

The nice old lady was angry as she re-entered the pet shop.

"That parrot I bought yesterday uses terrible language."

"That's right, lady," said the clerk, soothingly. "He does swear a bit, but you ought to be thankful he doesn't drink or gamble."

"Describe the three kinds of blood vessels."
"Three kinds of blood vessels are arteries, veins and caterpillars."

Judge—"And what is this man charged with?"

Officer — "Intoxication, your honor."

Prisoner — "Judge, I'm as sober as you are."

Judge — "Prisoner pleads guilty — ten days! Next case!"

"I see in the paper that a widower with nine children out in Iowa has married a widow with seven children."

"That wasn't a marriage, that was a merger."

Two politicians chatting: "What do you look for in a new piece of legislation?"

"The greatest good to the greatest number."

"What do you consider the greatest number?"

"Number one."

"Bill's wife always laughs at his jokes."
"They must be pretty clever."
"No — she is."

Will — "She treated me badly."
Bill — "She treated me worse."
Will — "Impossible! She jilted me."
Bill — "She married *me*."

"Let's have a friendly game of cards?"
"No, let's play bridge."

"Lizzy swears that she has never been kissed by a man!"
"Well, isn't that enough to make any girl swear?"

An adult is a person who has stopped growing except in the middle.

A nut shop displays this sign: "If our peanuts were any fresher, they'd be insulting."

"What's worse than raining cats and dogs?"
"I don't know, unless maybe hailing busses."

A stingy man went into a butcher shop and asked for a quarter-pound of steak.
"But my dear man," said the butcher, "you've got nine children. What are you going to do with such a tiny piece of steak?"
"This ain't for eating," explained the customer. "I just like to have the smell of steak in the house when company comes."

Busy Boss — "I can't see you now, you'll have to arrange with my secretary for an appointment."
Salesman — "I tried to, but she's booked for two weeks ahead."

"What is a mayor?"
"A mayor is a she horse."

All brutes are imperfect animals. Man alone is a perfect beast.

"The radio will never take the place of newspapers."
"Why?"
"You can't start a fire with a radio set."

Etiquette is yawning with your mouth closed.

"Mother, you're not nearly so pretty as Nurse."
"Don't you think so, dear?"
"No. We've been walking round the park for an hour and not a single policeman has kissed you!"

21

"My Gawd, partner, what did you bid no trump on? I had three aces and all four kings."
"Well, if you really want to know — one jack, two queens and four drinks."

In front of the cathedral there was a man dressed in the garbage of a monk.

Visitor — "Well, Bill, how do you like your baby sister?"

Bill — "Oh, she's all right, but there are lots of things we needed more."

A teacher called for sentences using the word "beans."

"My father grows beans," said one farmer's child.

"My mother cooks beans," said another pupil.

Then a third answered: "We are all human beans."

Teacher — "Sonny, why are you late for school every morning?"

Pupil — "Every time I come to the corner a sign says, 'School — Go Slow.'"

A doctor told his patient that there was nothing really the matter with him. "All you need to tone you up is more outdoor life; say walking two or three miles every day. What's your business?"

"I'm a letter-carrier, doc."

The village doctor had two children, and everyone said they were the prettiest girls in town.

"Say," said a visitor, "who are those pretty little girls?"

"They're the doctor's children," said a village boy. "He always keeps the best for himself."

Teacher — "What is an octopus?"
Pupil — "An eight-sided cat."

"Johnny," said the teacher, "why don't you wash your face? I can see what you had for breakfast this morning."

"What did I have, teacher?"

"Eggs."

"You're wrong, teacher. That was yesterday."

"Mother, I just took a splinter out of my hand with a pin."

"A pin! Don't you know that's dangerous?"

"Oh, no, Mother, I used a safety pin."

A sure-footed man is a man that when he kicks you does not miss.

An antidote is a funny story that you have heard before.

Dentist — "Open wider please — wider."
Patient — "A-A-A-Ah."
Dentist (inserting rubber gag, towel and sponge) — "How's your family?"

Lady (to instructor) — "Don't you find that horseback riding gives one a headache?"
Instructor — "Oh, no lady; quite the opposite!"

Doctor — "I have to report, sir, that you are the father of triplets."
Politician — "Impossible! I'll demand a recount."

Dear Mabel: When we got there our trunk hadn't arrived, so we had to sleep in something else.

Quinine is the bark of a tree: canine is the bark of a dog.

"None of these dirty little jobs for me,"
said the college graduate, "I want to do
something big and something clean."
"Then wash an elephant."

"How are cathedrals supported?"
"Mediaeval cathedrals were supported
by flying buttocks."

Three deaf Englishmen were on a train for London. "I beg pardon, but what station is this?" asked the first.

"Wembley," answered the conductor.

"Heavens!" said the second. "I thought it was Thursday!"

"So am I," exclaimed the third. "Let's all go into the restaurant car and have a drink!"

Freshman — "But I really don't think I deserve a zero."

Prof. — "Neither do I, but it is the lowest grade I'm allowed to give."

Wife — "I've bought you a beautiful surprise for your birthday."

Husband — "Let's see it."

Wife — "Wait a minute till I put it on."

"Hello! Is this the city bridge department?"

"Yes! What can we do for you?"

"Tell me: how many points do I get for a little slam, doubled, vulnerable?"

One of the girls was wearing an engagement ring, but no one at the office noticed it. Finally in the afternoon, when some of the other typists were nearby, she stood up suddenly.

"My, it's hot in here," she said. "I think I'll take off my ring."

"Why did you leave your job?"
"Illness. The boss got sick of me."

Teacher (to little girl learning to write) — "But where is the dot over the i?"
Girl — "It's still in the pencil!"

"How did your wife get on with her reducing diet?"
"Great! — she disappeared completely last week!"

A Boston brokerage house advertised for "a young Harvard graduate or the equivalent." Among the answers was one from a Yale man: "When you speak of an equivalent," he wrote, "do you mean two Princeton men or a Yale man half-time?"

Advice to farmers: To keep milk from turning sour you should keep it in the cow.

First Egyptian — "Who was that lady I saw you with last night?"
Second Egyptian — "That was no lady. That was my mummy."

The minister looked at Mr. Willoughby sadly and said, "I'm told you went to the ball game Sunday, instead of going to church."
"That's a lie," cried Mr. Willoughby, "and I've got the fish to prove it."

"In politics, what is a revolution?"
"A revolution is a form of government abroad."

In a gay and carefree mood, a man telephoned to a friend at two o'clock in the morning. "I do hope I haven't disturbed you," he said cheerily.
"Oh, no," the friend replied. "I had to get up to answer the telephone anyway."

Judge — "Why did you steal the necklace from the jeweler's window?"

Prisoner — "A card on it said: 'Avail yourself of this splendid opportunity,' and I couldn't resist!"

"What is Spain's national musical instrument?" "Cascarets."

"You say the water that you get here is unsafe? Tell me, just what precautions do you take against it?"

"First we filter it, then we boil it, then we chlorinate it."

"Yes."

"Then we drink beer."

Midwestern tourist (to Vermont farmer) — "Where did all these rocks come from?"

Farmer — "Glacier brought 'em."

Tourist — "Where's the glacier now?"

Farmer — "Went back for more rocks."

Mrs. Newlywed — "I'm terribly sorry, dear, but dinner is a little burnt tonight."

Mr. Newlywed — "What? Was there a fire at the delicatessen?"

After much urging from her mother, a little girl wrote the following thank-you note: "Thank you for your nice present. I always wanted a pin cushion, although not very much."

A new father was away from home and received his glad tidings in a telegram: "Hazel gave birth to a little girl this morning; both doing well."

And on the message there was a sticker reading: "When you want a boy call Western Union."

Pupil — "Do you think it's right to punish people for things they haven't done?"

Teacher — "Why, of course not!"

Pupil — "Well, I haven't done my home work."

Medical Professor — "What would you prescribe for a man who had eaten poisonous mushrooms?"

Student — "A change of diet."

"Where's Bill?" asked a neighbor boy one winter afternoon.

"Well," said Bill's brother, "if the ice is as thick as he thinks it is, he's skating. But if it's as thin as I think it is, he's swimming."

"I have told your wife that she must go to the mountains."

"OK, doctor. Now tell *me* I must go to the seashore."

After her first horseback ride, a young lady was heard to make this comment: "I never imagined anything filled with hay could feel so hard!"

"What is Vesuvius?"

"Vesuvius is a volcano and if you will climb up to the top you will see the creator smoking."

Wife to Husband: "Remember that unbreakable toy you gave Mary yesterday?"

"I certainly do," he said. "Don't tell me she's broken it already?"

"Not at all," said the mother. "But she's broken all her other toys with it."

The Eskimos are God's frozen people.

A mountain range is a cooking stove made specially for use at high altitudes.

Film Producer (as he enters studio) — "Who's that?"

Director — "That's Napoleon."

Producer — "Why did you get such a little man to play such an important part?"

"Describe bamboo." "An Italian baby."

"You should meet my husband. He makes a living with his pen."

"Oh, so he's a writer?"

"No, he raises pigs."

Woman to husband as she arrives in auto with smashed fender: "And the policeman was so nice about it. He asked if I'd like for the city to remove all the telephone poles."

A girl applying for a job said she had won several prizes in crossword-puzzle and slogan-writing contests.

"Sounds good," the employer told her, "but we want somebody who will be smart during office hours."

"Oh," said the girl, "this *was* during office hours."

For the first time in her life the dear old lady had a telephone installed.

Soon she dialed the operator. "I wonder if you would help me out," she said. "My telephone wire is a little long, and gets caught in the sweeper. Would you pull it back a little from your end?"

"What is the plural of man, Oscar?" asked the teacher.
"Men," answered Oscar.
"And the plural of child?"
"Twins."

"How many times must I tell you, Willie, that you must keep your eyes closed during prayer."
"Yes, Mamma, but how do you know I don't?"

"Believe it or not, but when I see red I'm happy."
"How's that?"
"I sell a sunburn remedy."

Little Mary — "What is your new brother's name?"
Little Sally — "I don't know yet. I can't understand a word he says."

Mother — "What do you want to take your cod liver oil with, today, Junior?"
Junior — "With a fork."

Teacher — "John, what is a cannibal?"
John — "Don't know, Miss Tweet."
Teacher — "If you ate your father and mother, what would you be?"
John — "An orphan, Miss Tweet."

A momentum is what you give to a person when they are going away.

"Define a circle."
"A circle is a round line with no kinks in it, joined up so as not to show where it began."

"Dear Miss Fairfax: How should a lady walk with a gentleman?"
"When a lady and a gentleman are walking on the sidewalk the lady should walk inside the gentleman."

Mabel — "What's the matter with your feet?"
Dora — "I've got corns."
Mabel — "Why don't you do something for them?"
Dora — "Why should I? They've never done anything for me."

"Why was Solomon the wisest man in the world?"
"Because he had so many wives to tell him what to do."

"What is the function of the stomach?"
"The function of the stomach is to hold up the pants."

"Why does this meat taste so queer?" asked the young husband.

"I can't imagine," replied his bride, "I burned it a little but I put sunburn oil on it at once."

Wife, showing a new hat to her husband: "It didn't cost a thing, dear. It was marked down from $20 to $10, so I bought it with the $10 I saved!"

One starlet was telling another that she bought all her Christmas presents in October.

"But how do you know in October," exclaimed the other, "who your friends are going to be in December?"

A young sailor came home on leave and said: "Dad, I need your help. I've got to get something off my chest."

"Oh," his father said. "Tell me."

The sailor said: "I'm going to marry Joan, but I've got to get this off my chest." He opened his shirt, and there on his chest was tattooed: "I love Fifi."

"Johnny, the canary has disappeared."
"That's funny. It was there just now when I tried to clean it with the vacuum-cleaner."

Son — "What is a lawyer?"
Father — "A lawyer is a man who urges two other men to strip for a fight, and then runs off with their clothes."

"Do you believe in clubs for women?"
"Yes," said the bearded man, "if every other form of persuasion fails."

A lady was mailing a Bible. The postal clerk asked if the package contained anything breakable. "Only the Ten Commandments," said the lady.

Landlady — "Do you want a room?"
Room-hunter — "No, I want to make believe I'm a banana and sleep in the fruit dish."

"She was only the optician's daughter — two glasses and she made a spectacle of herself."

Child — "Mother, may I have a nickel for the old man who is outside crying?"
Mother — "Yes, dear, but what is the old man crying about?"
Child — "He's crying, 'Peanuts, five cents a bag.'"

The Rumba is a dance where the front of you goes along smooth like a Cadillac and the back of you shakes like a Model T.

They arrived late for a baseball game — just in time for the fifth inning.
"What's the score, Jim?" he asked a friend.
"Nothing to nothing," was the reply.
"Oh, goody!" she exclaimed. "Then we haven't missed a thing!"

A brazier is a kind of garment people used to wear instead of having their houses heated by steam heat.

"What do we do when we breathe?"
"When you breathe you inspire. When you do not breathe you expire."

"Well," said the doctor to the housewife, "what is the matter with your husband? He looks worried."

"I think, doctor, he is worried about money."

"Well, you just send him in to me. I can relieve him of *that!*"

A hospital patient gazed fondly at his pretty red-headed nurse and told the doctor, "Wonderful nurse you've got here. One touch of her lovely hand cooled my fever."

"We know," the doctor answered. "We could hear her slap clear to the end of the corridor."

Doctor — "Well, my dear, you seem to have water on the knee. Now what had we better do?"
Patient — "Suppose, instead of flats, I wear pumps?"

A little boy showed his father a new penknife. He said he had found it in the street.

"Are you sure it was lost?" inquired the father.

"Of course, it was lost! I saw the man looking for it!" replied the boy.

"Did you tell Mr. Jones that his wife has just had triplets?"
"Didn't dare. He is still shaving."

A meek little man in a restaurant timidly touched the arm of a man putting on a coat. "Excuse me," he said, "but do you happen to be Mr. Milquetoast?"

"No, I'm not!" the man snapped.

"Well," said the first man, "you see, I *am* Mr. Milquetoast, and that's his overcoat you're putting on."

"What do you think of our two candidates for mayor?"
"Well, I'm glad only one of them can be elected."

A lady complained to a friend: "Elsie told me that you told her the secret I told you not to tell her."

"But," replied her friend indignantly, "I told her not to tell you I told her."

"Oh, dear," sighed the first.

"Well, don't you tell her I told you she told me."

"Do you believe marriage is a lottery?"
"No; in a lottery a man is supposed to have a chance."

"Did you go to the senator's funeral?"
"Sure did. They gave him a real great funeral. It took twelve men to carry the beer."

"Describe respiration."
"Respiration is composed of two acts, first comes inspiration and then comes expectoration."

Contralto is a low sort of music that only ladies sing.

A blonde told her best friend, "It's not true that I married a millionaire. I made him one."
"A likely story. And what was he *before* you married him?" asked the friend.
The wife: "A multi-millionaire."

"I think Willie is a bad egg."
"No, he's too fresh for that."

In Christianity a man can only have one wife. This is called Monotony.

"Did you ever hear the story about the peacock?"
"No."
"A beautiful tale!"

"Is man an animal?"
"Yes: man is an animal split half way up and walks on the split end."

The doctor was questioning the new nurse about her patient. "Have you kept a chart of his progress?"

The nurse replied with a blush, "No, but I can show you my diary."

Policeman — "So you're lost, little man? Why didn't you hang onto your mother's skirt?"

Youngster — "I couldn't reach it."

"Doris could have married anybody she pleased."

"Then why is she still single?"

"She never pleased anybody."

"Did you hear about the awful fright George got on his wedding day?"

"Oh, yes; I was there. I saw her."

Mother — "Willie-e-e! What's your brother crying about? Didn't I tell you to give him anything he wanted?"

Willie — "Yes, Ma; but I've dug him a hole, and now he wants me to bring it in the house."

Mary — "What do you say to a tramp in the woods?"
Jane — "I never speak to strange men."

"You complain that you have had to support your wife's family?" the judge questioned the man seeking a divorce.
"Yes, your honor."
"How much of a family has she?"
"Four children, your honor."
"Who is their father?"
"I am, your honor."

"Are you homesick?" her aunt asked a small girl, away for the first time overnight.
"No," the child sobbed. "I'm here sick."

"This liniment makes my arm smart."
"Better rub some on your head!"

"I saw Brown the other day treating his wife the way I wouldn't treat a dog."
"What was he doing?"
"Kissing her."

Wife — "I can't decide whether to go to a palm-reader or to a mind-reader."

Husband — "Go to a palm-reader. I'm sure you have a palm."

Driver — "Some of you pedestrians act like you owned the streets."

Walker — "Yes, and some of you drivers act like you owned your cars."

"Is New York time earlier or later than Greenwich time?"

"New York time is behind Greenwich time because America was not discovered until later."

The dirty old jalopy wheezed up to the toll-bridge.

"Fifty cents," cried the toll-taker.

"Sold," replied the driver.

"Johnny, what is the equator?"

"The equator is a menagerie lion running round the earth and through Africa."

"Where is the population of this country densest?"
"That's an easy one, brother, — from the neck up!"

The greatest miracle in the Bible is when Joshua told his son to stand still and he obeyed him.

Nurse — "Doctor, there's a man outside who says he has a dual personality."
"Tell him to go chase himself."

"My dumb brother is working with 2,000 men under him."
"Really?"
"Yep! He cuts the grass in a cemetery."

"Hey, look — the barometer's falling!"
"Too bad, — probably wasn't nailed up right."

"What is the difference between weather and climate?"
"Climate lasts all the time, but weather only a few days."

"Did you hear Simmons snoring away in church this morning? It was simply awful."
"Yes, I did — he woke me up."

"I always tell my wife everything that happens."
"That's nothing. I tell my wife lots of things that never happen."

A famous lawyer refuses to go to dinner parties because too many people spoil his evening by asking for legal advice. He asked a doctor if this happened to him.
"Sure thing!" the doctor said.
"How do you get rid of them?"
"I have a wonderful remedy," the doctor said. "When they begin to tell me their ailments, I just say: 'Undress!'"

"Is ink expensive, father?"
"No. Why do you ask?"
"Because mother got so upset when I spilled a bottle of it on the living-room carpet."

Dickey — "My Dad is an Elk, a Lion, and a Moose."
Mickey — "What does it cost me to see him?"

Nurse — "Well, Sonny, you have a new baby brother for a Christmas present."
Sonny — "Oh, great! May I be the first to tell Mother?"

An old lady came to the door with a suitcase, and rang the bell. A little boy opened the door.
"You don't know me," said the old lady, "but I'm your grandmother — on your father's side."
The boy shook his head. "I'll tell you right now: you're on the wrong side."

Mrs. Jones (riffling through her newspaper) — "It says here that a woman in Pittsburgh has just cremated her third husband."
Miss Willing — "Heigho! Isn't that just the way? Some of us can't get one husband and other women have husbands to burn."

Tough (nicked by the barber's razor) — "Hey barber, gimme a glass of water."
Barber — "What's wrong, sir?"
Tough — "I wanna see if my neck leaks."

"Define a polygon."
"A polygon is a dead parrot."

✓ The bachelor-girl hooted when anyone suggested that it was too bad she did not have a husband.
"I have a dog that growls, a parrot that swears, a fireplace that smokes, and a cat that stays out all night. Why should I want a husband?"

"Miss Smith," said the physics professor, "would you tell the class what happens when a body is immersed in water?"
"Usually," said Miss Smith, "The telephone rings."

A skeleton is a man with his inside out and his outside off.

Farmer Jones was boasting again. "I am a real old-fashioned farmer," he said. "I can plow, reap, milk cows, shoe a horse — in fact, I should like for someone to tell me one thing about a farm which I cannot do."

Then, in the impressive silence, a voice asked: "Can you lay an egg?"

"If the Dean doesn't take back what he said to me this morning, I am going to leave college."
"What did he say?"
"He told me to leave college."

A drunken cowboy rushed into a bar, shooting his revolver, and yelling, "All you dirty rats get outta here."
The customers fled in a hail of bullets — all except an English tourist, who sat at his table calmly finishing his drink.
The cowboy came over to him. "I said, all dirty rats get outta here!"
"Yes," said the Englishman, "and there certainly were a lot of them, weren't there!"

Admirer — "I'd love to be married to you some day."
Screen Star — "All right, I'll put you on my wedding list."

Asked if he liked smart girls, the gay young man replied: "I like a girl with a good head on my shoulder."

A man bought a canary from a pet store. "You're absolutely sure this bird can sing?" he asked.

"He's a wonderful singer."

A week later the customer reappeared. "Say! This bird you sold me is lame!"

"Well, you said you wanted a singer, not a dancer."

Mother — "What did Daddy say when he saw the bill for my new hat?"

Son — "Should I leave out the dirty words?"

Mother — "Of course leave out the dirty words! What did he say?"

Son — "Nuthin'!"

Lady (in a pet shop) — "I like this dog, but his legs are too short."

Salesman — "Too short! Why, madam, they all four touch the floor."

Patient — "My wife tells me I walk in my sleep, doctor. What should I do?"

Doctor — "Nothing you shouldn't."

Correct this sentence: "It was me who broke the window."
"It wasn't me who broke the window."

"My horse knows as much as I do."
"Well, don't tell anybody. You may want to sell him some day."

Dave — "I can tell you the score of any baseball game before it starts."
Joe — "What is it?"
Dave — "Nothing to nothing."

"Is the doctor in?" inquired the caller.
"Nope," answered his little boy.
"Do you know when he'll be back?"
"Nope — he went on an eternity case."

Mother — "Wash your hands for dinner."
Son — "They aren't really dirty — just kinda blurred."

"Define parallel lines."
"Parallel lines never meet unless you bend one or both of them."

Bill — "What's the best way to teach a girl to swim?"

Bob — "First you put your left arm around her waist, then you gently take her right hand and —"

Bill — "She's my sister."

Bob — "Oh — push her off the dock."

A monologue is a conversation between two people, such as a husband and wife.

Sam — "Say, my wooden leg pained me terribly last night."

Joe — "How's that?"

Sam — "My wife hit me over the head with it."

Two straight lines cannot enclose a space unless they are crooked.

"What is the difference between an optimist and a pessimist?"

"An optimist is a man who looks after your eyes, a pessimist looks after your feet."

A five-year-old was watching his mother change the baby. When she forgot to sprinkle the baby with talcum, and hurried him into his diaper, the five-year-old said, "Hey, Mom, you forgot to salt him!"

The congressman's wife sat up in bed, a startled look on her face. "Jim," she whispered, "there's a robber in the house."

"Impossible," was her husband's sleepy reply. "In the Senate, yes, but in the House, never."

Rose — "What is your worst sin?"
Daisy — "My vanity. I spend hours before the mirror admiring my beauty."
Rose — "That isn't vanity, dear — that's imagination."

Doctor Son — "Well, Dad, now that I'm hanging out my shingle, give me some rules for success."
Doctor Father — "Always write your prescriptions illegibly. Always write your bills legibly."

It was early afternoon. At the movie house the box-office girl asked the boy, "Why aren't you in school?"

"Oh, it's all right," said he. "I've got measles."

"Daddy, what's a 'feebly'?"
"A 'feebly'?"
"Yes, Daddy."
"How's it used?"
"Why, here in this book it says, 'The man had a feebly growing down on his chin.'"

Pullman passenger — "Say porter, what about these shoes? You've brought me back one black and one brown!"
Porter — "Well, if it don't beat all! It's the second time that's happened this morning!"

"Say, does your wife play bridge for money?"
"Maybe she plays for it, but she never gets any."

"Beastly weather we're having, isn't it? — It's raining cats and dogs."

"Name six animals from the Arctic regions."
"Three bears and three seals."

"A moth leads an awful life."
"How come?"
"He spends the summer in a fur coat and the winter in a bathing suit."

"Describe latitude and longitude."
"Latitude tells you how hot you are, and longitude how cold you are."

Irene — "How old would you say she is?"
Sally — "Oh, somewhere in the middle flirties!"

"He isn't so bad, but he sure is bigoted."
"How do you mean?"
"He thinks words should be spelled one way and one way only!"